POEMS BY

WILLIAM WORDSWORTH
ROBERT LOUIS STEVENSON
WALT WHITMAN
EMILY BRONTË
SARAH TEASDALE

SA.
NURIA TAMARIT
JOE TODD STANTON
PEP BOATELLA
SAM LEDOYEN
EMILY KIMBELL

I Wandered Lonely as a Cloud and other poems

Contents

OXFORD
UNIVERSITY PRESS

I Wandered Lonely as a Cloud
By William Wordsworth

I wandered lonely as a cloud

That floats on high o'er vales and hills,

When all at once I saw a crowd,
A host, of golden daffodils;

Beside the lake, beneath the trees,
Fluttering and dancing in the breeze.

Continuous as the stars that shine
And twinkle on the milky way,

They stretched in never-ending line
Along the margin of a bay:

Ten thousand saw I at a glance,
Tossing their heads in sprightly dance.

The waves beside them danced; but they
Out-did the sparkling waves in glee:-

A poet could not but be gay,
In such a jocund company:

I gazed – and gazed – but little thought

What wealth the show to me had brought:

For oft when on my couch I lie
In vacant or in pensive mood,

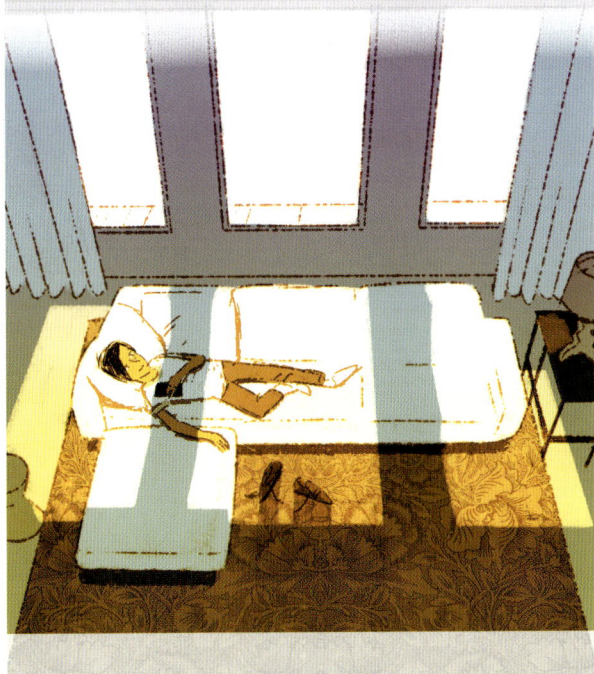

They flash upon that inward eye
Which is the bliss of solitude,

And then my heart with pleasure fills,

And dances with the daffodils.

I Wandered Lonely as a Cloud
By William Wordsworth

I wandered lonely as a cloud
That floats on high o'er vales and hills,
When all at once I saw a crowd,
A host, of golden daffodils;
Beside the lake, beneath the trees,
Fluttering and dancing in the breeze.

Continuous as the stars that shine
And twinkle on the milky way,
They stretched in never-ending line
Along the margin of a bay:
Ten thousand saw I at a glance,
Tossing their heads in sprightly dance.

The waves beside them danced; but they
Out-did the sparkling waves in glee:-
A poet could not but be gay
In such a jocund company:
I gazed – and gazed – but little thought
What wealth the show to me had brought:

For oft when on my couch I lie
In vacant or in pensive mood,
They flash upon that inward eye
Which is the bliss of solitude,
And then my heart with pleasure fills,
And dances with the daffodils.

William Wordsworth was born in 1770. He grew up in the Lake District, a very picturesque area of northern England, which sparked his lifelong love of nature.

William began writing poetry while he was at school. He studied at Cambridge University and enjoyed going on walking holidays during the summer break.

William and his sister Dorothy were good friends with another poet, Samuel Taylor Coleridge. William and Samuel wrote a famous collection of poems together, called *Lyrical Ballads*, which was published in 1798.

William had five children with his wife Mary, although two died before adulthood. William was made Poet Laureate in 1843, and he died in 1850.

The Wind

By Robert Louis Stevenson

I saw you toss the kites on high

And blow the birds about the sky;

And all around I heard you pass,
Like ladies' skirts across the grass—

O wind, a-blowing all day long,
O wind, that sings so loud a song!

I saw the different things you did,
But always you yourself you hid.

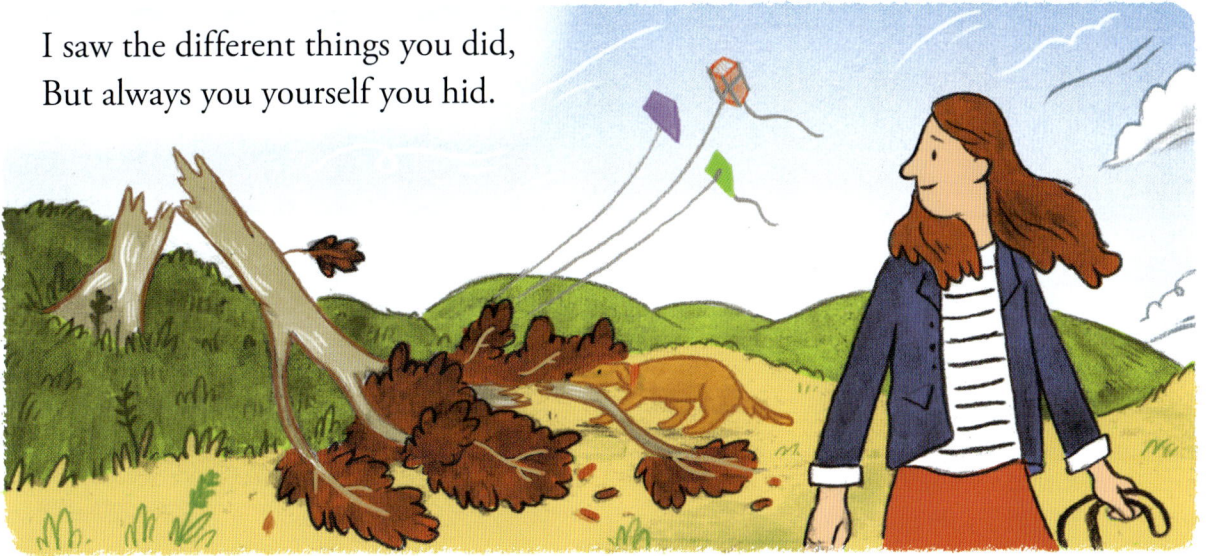

I felt you push, I heard you call,
I could not see yourself at all—

O wind, a-blowing all day long,
O wind, that sings so loud a song!

O you that are so strong and cold,
O blower, are you young or old?

Are you a beast of field and tree,
Or just a stronger child than me?

O wind, a-blowing all day long,
O wind, that sings so loud a song!

The Wind

By Robert Louis Stevenson

I saw you toss the kites on high
And blow the birds about the sky;
And all around I heard you pass,
Like ladies' skirts across the grass—
 O wind, a-blowing all day long,
 O wind, that sings so loud a song!

I saw the different things you did,
But always you yourself you hid.
I felt you push, I heard you call,
I could not see yourself at all—
 O wind, a-blowing all day long,
 O wind, that sings so loud a song!

O you that are so strong and cold,
O blower, are you young or old?
Are you a beast of field and tree,
Or just a stronger child than me?
 O wind, a-blowing all day long,
 O wind, that sings so loud a song!

Pirate Story
Robert Louis Stevenson

Three of us afloat in the meadow by the swing,

Three of us abroad in the basket on the lea.

Winds are in the air, they are blowing in the spring,
And waves are on the meadow like the waves there are at sea.

Where shall we adventure, to-day that we're afloat,
Wary of the weather and steering by a star?

Shall it be to Africa, a-steering of the boat,
To Providence, or Babylon, or off to Malabar?

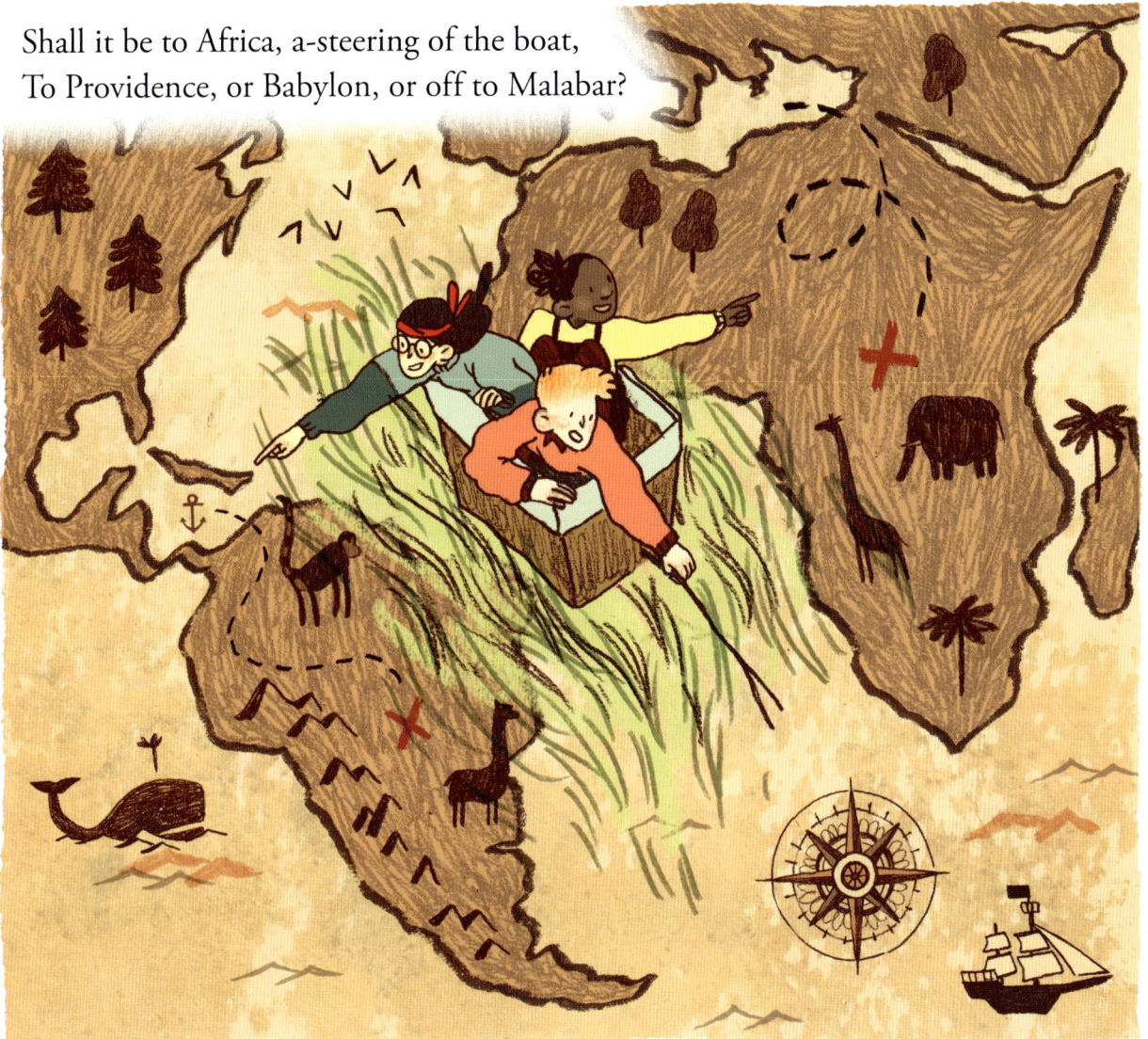

Hi! but here's a squadron a-rowing on the sea—
Cattle on the meadow a-charging with a roar!

Quick, and we'll escape them, they're as mad as they can be,
The wicket is the harbour and the garden is the shore.

Pirate Story
By Robert Louis Stevenson

Three of us afloat in the meadow by the swing,
   Three of us abroad in the basket on the lea.
Winds are in the air, they are blowing in the spring,
   And waves are on the meadow like the waves there are at sea.

Where shall we adventure, to-day that we're afloat,
   Wary of the weather and steering by a star?
Shall it be to Africa, a-steering of the boat,
   To Providence, or Babylon, or off to Malabar?

Hi! but here's a squadron a-rowing on the sea—
   Cattle on the meadow a-charging with a roar!
Quick, and we'll escape them, they're as mad as they can be,
   The wicket is the harbour and the garden is the shore.

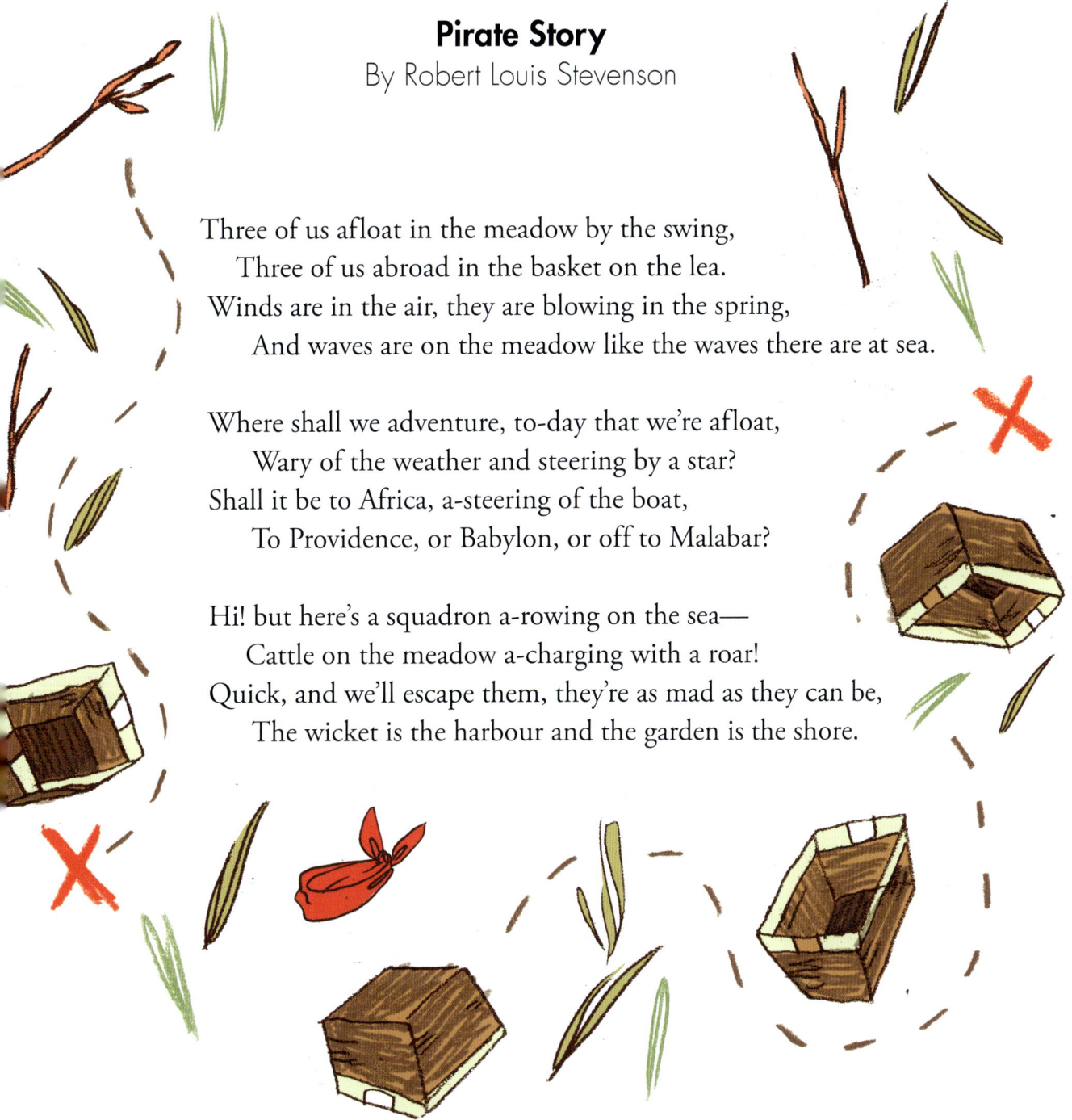

Bed in Summer
By Robert Louis Stevenson

In winter I get up at night
And dress by yellow candle-light.

In summer quite the other way,
I have to go to bed by day.

I have to go to bed and see
The birds still hopping on the tree,

Or hear the grown-up people's feet
Still going past me in the street.

And does it not seem hard to you,
When all the sky is clear and blue,
And I should like so much to play,
To have to go to bed by day?

Bed in Summer
By Robert Louis Stevenson

In winter I get up at night
And dress by yellow candle-light.
In summer quite the other way,
I have to go to bed by day.

I have to go to bed and see
The birds still hopping on the tree,
Or hear the grown-up people's feet
Still going past me in the street.

And does it not seem hard to you,
When all the sky is clear and blue,
And I should like so much to play,
To have to go to bed by day?

Robert Louis Stevenson was born in Edinburgh, Scotland, in 1850. He began writing stories as a child. He studied engineering at college, but he didn't want to be a lighthouse designer like his father and grandfather. Instead, he became a writer.

He was often ill with a chest complaint, and he travelled to warm places to try to get better. Eventually he moved to the South Pacific island of Samoa, where he died in 1894.

He wrote about forty books in total. Robert is best known for his novels *Treasure Island*, *The Strange Case of Dr Jekyll and Mr Hyde* and *Kidnapped*.

The World Below the Brine

By Walt Whitman

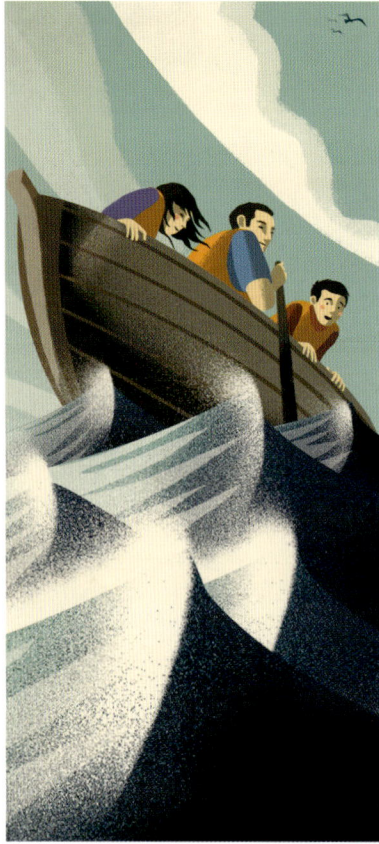

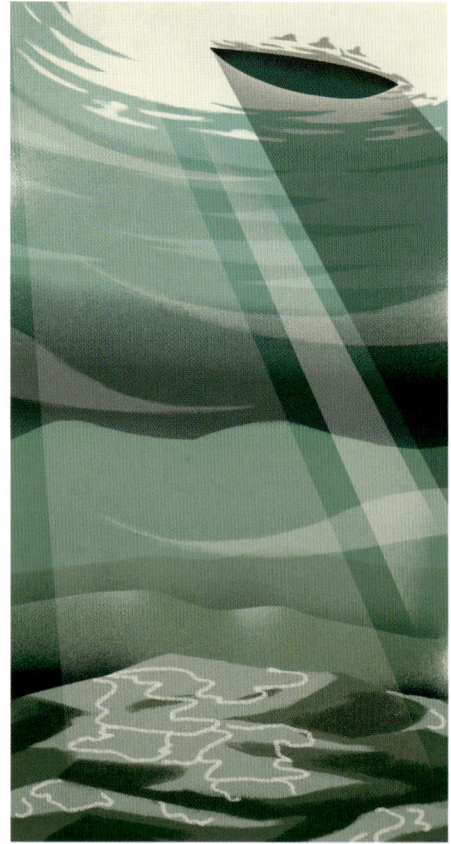

The world below the brine,
Forests at the bottom of the sea, the branches and leaves,
Sea-lettuce, vast lichens, strange flowers and seeds,
 the thick tangle, openings, and pink turf,

Different colours, pale grey and green, purple, white,
and gold, the play of light through the water,

Dumb swimmers there among the rocks, coral, gluten,
grass, rushes, and the aliment of the swimmers,
Sluggish existences grazing there suspended, or slowly
crawling close to the bottom,

The sperm-whale at the surface blowing air and
spray, or disporting with his flukes,

The leaden-eyed shark, the walrus, the turtle,
the hairy sea-leopard, and the sting-ray,

Passions there, wars, pursuits, tribes, sight in those ocean-depths,
    breathing that thick-breathing air, as so many do,

The change thence to the sight here, and to the subtle air breathed by
    beings like us who walk this sphere,

The change onward from ours to that of beings who walk other spheres.

The World Below the Brine
By Walt Whitman

The world below the brine,
Forests at the bottom of the sea, the branches and leaves,
Sea-lettuce, vast lichens, strange flowers and seeds,
    the thick tangle, openings, and pink turf,
Different colours, pale grey and green, purple, white,
    and gold, the play of light through the water,
Dumb swimmers there among the rocks, coral, gluten,
    grass, rushes, and the aliment of the swimmers,
Sluggish existences grazing there suspended, or slowly
    crawling close to the bottom,
The sperm-whale at the surface blowing air and
    spray, or disporting with his flukes,
The leaden-eyed shark, the walrus, the turtle,
    the hairy sea-leopard, and the sting-ray,
Passions there, wars, pursuits, tribes, sight in those ocean-depths,
    breathing that thick-breathing air, as so many do,
The change thence to the sight here, and to the subtle air breathed by
    beings like us who walk this sphere,
The change onward from ours to that of beings who walk other spheres.

Walt Whitman was born in America in 1819, to a Dutch mother and English father. It was a large family as Walt had eight siblings. The family were poor, so they moved to Brooklyn, New York, in the hope of better opportunities.

Walt left school at eleven and began working for a printer. When he was older he became a successful journalist and newspaper editor.

He couldn't find a publisher for his first collection of poetry, *Leaves of Grass*, so he printed it himself. It was later translated into many different languages.

During the American Civil War, Walt visited soldiers from both sides of the war in hospital, bringing small gifts to cheer them up.

Throughout his life, Walt enjoyed reading, theatre and music. He died in 1892.

Past, Present, Future

By Emily Brontë

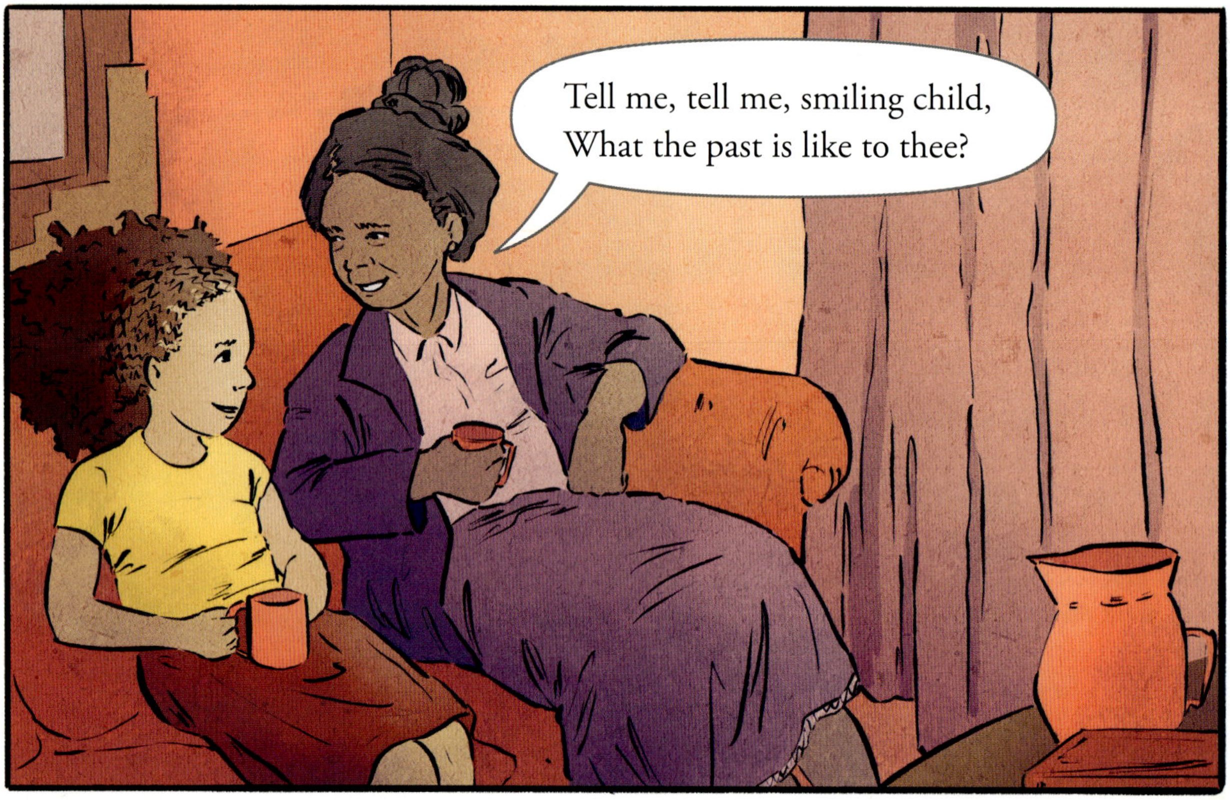

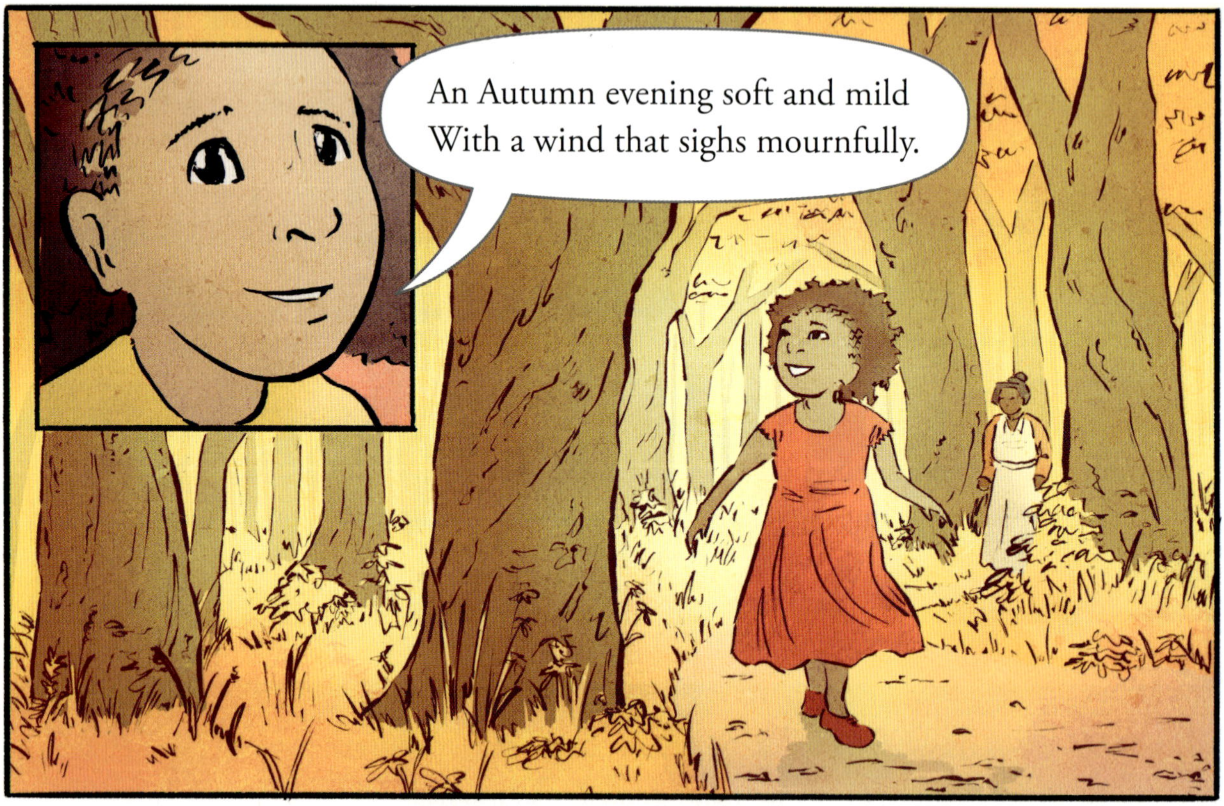

Past, Present, Future
By Emily Brontë

Tell me, tell me, smiling child,
What the past is like to thee?
'An Autumn evening soft and mild
With a wind that sighs mournfully.'

Tell me, what is the present hour?
'A green and flowery spray
Where a young bird sits gathering its power
To mount and fly away.'

And what is the future, happy one?
'A sea beneath a cloudless sun;
A mighty, glorious, dazzling sea
Stretching into infinity.'

Emily Brontë was born in 1818 in Yorkshire, England. She was deeply inspired by her surroundings, and the Yorkshire moors feature throughout her writing.

Emily worked as a teacher and a governess, before moving to Brussels for a short time to improve her French.

One day, her sister Charlotte accidentally found some of Emily's poetry that she'd kept a secret. So along with their other sister, Anne, they wrote and published a book of poetry together. Charlotte and Anne also went on to write novels individually.

Emily used the name 'Ellis Bell' to initially publish her work. She is best known for her only novel *Wuthering Heights*, which is set in Yorkshire. She died in 1848 at the age of thirty.

The Falling Star
By Sara Teasdale

I saw a star slide down the sky,
Blinding the north as it went by,

Too burning and too quick to hold,
Too lovely to be bought or sold,

Good only to make wishes on
And then forever to be gone.

The Falling Star
By Sara Teasdale

I saw a star slide down the sky,
Blinding the north as it went by,
Too burning and too quick to hold,
Too lovely to be bought or sold,
Good only to make wishes on
And then forever to be gone.

About Sara Teasdale

Sara Teasdale was born in Missouri, America, in 1884. She started writing poetry at an early age and spent a lot of time in Chicago, where she knew many other poets. Sara had her first poem published when she was twenty-two years old.

In 1914, Sara married. She moved with her husband to New York in 1916. In 1918, she won the Columbia University Poetry Society prize.

Sara died in 1933. Her final poetry collection, *Strange Victory*, was published posthumously (after her death) that year.